The I

Florian Zeller is a French novelist and playwright. He won the prestigious Prix Interallié in 2004 for his third novel, *Fascination of Evil*. His plays include *L'Autre, Le Manège, Si tu mourais, Elle t'attend* and *La Vérité, La Mère* (*The Mother*, Molière Award for Best Play in 2011) and *Le Père* (*The Father*, Molière Award for Best Play in 2014), starring Robert Hirsch and Isabelle Gelinas (Molière Awards for Best Actor and Actress, Prix du Brigadier in 2015). *Une Heure de tranquillité* (*A Bit of Peace and Quiet*) opened with Fabrice Luchini, and has since been adapted for the screen, directed by Patrice Leconte. *Le Mensonge* (*The Lie*) was staged in 2015 and *L'Envers du décor* opened in January 2016 at the Théâtre de Paris, starring Daniel Auteuil, and *Avant de s'envoler* (*The Height of the Storm*) at the Théâtre de l'Oeuvre in October 2016. His most recent play, *The Son*, completing his 'Family Trilogy', was produced in Paris in 2018 (Molière nomination) and will have its London premiere at the Kiln Theatre in Spring 2019.

Christopher Hampton was born in the Azores in 1946. He wrote his first play, *When Did You Last See My Mother?*, at the age of eighteen. Since then, his plays have included *The Philanthropist, Savages, Tales from Hollywood, Les Liaisons Dangereuses, White Chameleon, The Talking Cure* and *Appomattox*. He has translated plays by Ibsen, Molière, von Horváth, Chekhov and Yasmina Reza. His television work includes adaptations of *The History Man* and *Hôtel du Lac*. His screenplays include *The Honorary Consul, The Good Father, Dangerous Liaisons, Mary Reilly, Total Eclipse, The Quiet American, Atonement, Cheri, A Dangerous Method, Carrington, The Secret Agent* and *Imagining Argentina*, the last three of which he also directed.

FLORIAN ZELLER

The Height of the Storm

translated by
CHRISTOPHER HAMPTON

FABER & FABER

First published in 2018
by Faber and Faber Limited
74–77 Great Russell Street, London WC1B 3DA

Typeset by Country Setting, Kingsdown, Kent CT14 8ES
Printed and bound by CPI Group (UK) Ltd, Croydon, CR0 4YY

René Char, 'Au plus fort de l'orage . . . ' from 'Rougeur des Matinaux'
in *Les Matinaux* © Editions Gallimard, Paris, 1950

Henri Michaux, extracts from 'Contre !' in *La nuit remue*
© Editions Gallimard, Paris, 1967

A CIP record for this book is available from the British Library

ISBN 978-0-571-35058-2

8 10 9

The Height of the Storm in this translation by Christopher Hampton was first presented by Simon Friend, Mark Goucher and Howard Panter at the Richmond Theatre on 1 September 2018, and in the West End at Wyndham's Theatre on 6 October 2018. The cast was as follows:

André Jonathan Pryce
Madeleine Eileen Atkins
Anne Amanda Drew
Élise Anna Madeley
A Woman Lucy Cohu
A Man James Hillier

Direction Jonathan Kent
Set Design Anthony Ward
Lighting Design Hugh Vanstone
Sound Design Paul Groothuis

Avant de s'envoler in its original French production opened at the Théâtre de l'Oeuvre, Paris, on 5 October 2016, directed by Ladislas Chollat, with Robert Hirsch and Isabelle Sadoyan.

Characters

Anne
daughter

André
father

Madeleine
mother

Élise
second daughter

A Woman

A Man

THE HEIGHT OF THE STORM

One

A house. The drawing room opens on to a kitchen. André is looking out of the window, as if watching out for someone.

Anne What are you looking at? Did you hear that storm last night? It woke me up. Didn't it wake you? It's a long time since I've seen such a violent storm. It was impressive. Don't you think?

Pause.

What is it you're looking at? Come and sit down . . .

André doesn't move.

It's no use just standing there, you know.

Pause. She goes up to him and glances out of the window, as if she wanted to check what André is looking at, then moves off.

You ought to come and sit down. It's no use waiting.

Her gaze falls on André's old armchair; she smiles. She rests her hand on the back of it, as if she wanted to stroke it.

I'm thinking this was already here when I was a child. It was, wasn't it? This chair . . . All in all, nothing much has changed here . . .

Pause. She's hesitating about saying something to him, finally decides to take the plunge.

I was looking through your desk, you know, and I came across your diaries . . .

3

Pause. For the first time, André looks at her.

I didn't know you were still writing . . . I mean, these last few months . . .

Pause.

I don't know what to do with them . . . What would you do, if you were me?

Pause. He looks away again.

Anyway, there are so many heaps of paper to sort through . . . I don't know how you found your way around. I always feel compelled to tidy everything away . . . I can't bear mess. It upsets me. I don't know who I get that from . . . Because you and Mum are the complete opposite . . . Aren't you?

Summoning up this image causes a fragile smile, which disappears immediately.

But now all that needs organising. That's what I'm here for.

Pause.

No, I didn't sleep much last night. And not only because of the storm . . . Obviously. All this has disturbed me, you can imagine. And then there's the very fact of sleeping here. In my childhood bedroom. I think I must have slept there at least . . . I don't know. Ten years. Maybe even longer . . .

Pause.

At one point, when the rain had eased off, I got up and found myself here. All by myself. There wasn't a sound. And I stayed here. In the drawing room. I was thinking about you. About all the things we said to each other yesterday evening . . .

She turns to him.

You understand, we need to find some solution.

André turns towards her, his expression somewhat hostile.

(*Unconfidently.*) Of course, this is a wonderful house . . .
I don't deny it. We're all attached to it. But is it still what
the situation calls for?

*André abandons his position close to the window
and sets off towards his chair, moving slowly. His
annoyance is palpable.*

I mean . . . You can't live in this place on your own.
If you want to buy a loaf of bread, you have to take the
car . . .

André stops in his tracks.

It's just common sense, Dad. You can't live here on your
own.

André Croissants.

Anne What?

André I have croissants. Not bread.

Anne Yes, yes . . . I know. Same thing.

André Bread and croissants? The same thing?

Anne No. Obviously.

André So?

*He shrugs his shoulders, to demonstrate the
irrelevance of what his daughter's saying. And goes to
sit down.*

Anne What I meant is . . . the house is isolated. When
there were two of you, it was still viable. But now . . . it

might be time to come up with something else. A different configuration. Don't you think? With some things, you need to know when to let go. Sometimes.

The bell rings. She sees he hasn't reacted.

You want me to get that?

André It's quite simple. I have croissants, that's all. With butter. And jam. Strawberry jam, if you must know!

Anne Right. I . . . Don't move. I'll go.

She goes to the door.

André I dunk them in my coffee. At one time, I also used to like apricot jam. But that's a bygone age. Time has passed. Under the bridge. Except that nowadays who understands that? *Who* understands?

She comes back with a bunch of flowers, which has clearly just been delivered.

Anne Oh, look . . . Yet more flowers. See? It's really . . . There's no card. Strange . . . Do you know where the vases are kept? Two days now I've been searching for vases . . .

She starts to unwrap the flowers.

Anyway, they're beautiful. Don't you think? You've always loved flowers . . . I remember . . . Peonies were your favourite . . . You often used to buy them for Mum? She loved flowers as well . . . Didn't she? All the same, it's strange not to send a card with them. How do we know who sent them?

She glances at her father. She's still searching the cupboards for a vase. Pause. Then, cheerfully, as if she's trying to distract him.

I went for a walk yesterday. I went for a stroll round the town. I didn't know they'd put up that building . . . What is it? A sports centre? You know the building I mean? Opposite the Town Hall . . . Yes? It's really hideous. Don't you think? I sometimes wonder who makes these decisions. Ah, there's a vase . . .

She continues to arrange the flowers, very casual.

Anyway, on my walk, I passed an estate agent.

André reacts to this.

I dropped in and had a word with the man there. Charming fellow. And I explained the situation to him.

He doesn't understand what she's talking about.

The situation, Dad . . . I explained it to him. And he suggested calling round, to have a word with you about it. And also to get an idea of what might be involved . . .

He's glaring at her accusingly.

Obviously, you wouldn't be committed to anything. But we've been talking about it for such a long time without doing anything about it . . . So, as I'm here this weekend, I thought it might be a good opportunity . . . Don't you think? An opportunity to make some concrete progress.

Brief pause.

Anyway. He said he'd try to drop by tomorrow. Just for a visit. If you agree, of course.

André By the ton.

Anne (*who hasn't understood*) Sorry?

André By the ton!

Anne I . . . I don't know what you mean.

André (*as if to himself*) 'What you have denied me in grams, I will rip from you by the ton.'

Anne What . . . what are you saying?

André 'I will build you a city out of piles of rags, yes, I will. Without plans and without cement, I will build you a structure you can never destroy. Which will be supported and inflated by a kind of overflowing undeniability . . . I will install for you proud and overpowering fortresses. Fortresses made entirely from alarums and excursions . . . Toll the bell! Toll the bell! For all of you! Oblivion to the living!'

Anne is paralysed by this outburst from her father, which seems to come from beyond the grave. Suddenly, a key can be heard in the front door. A change of atmosphere. Anne returns to the real world. She turns: her mother appears, followed by her sister, Élise. They're back from the shops. Élise has carrier bags in both hands.

Madeleine What are you doing? Talking to yourself now?

Anne Mm? No. We . . . We were talking about the house. And we . . . In fact, I was arranging these flowers. They've just been delivered. There's no card with them.

Élise Really?

Anne No. I . . . I checked.

Élise Who sends flowers without a card? It's completely idiotic.

Anne You're right, I don't know. They're beautiful. Don't you think?

Madeleine I'm not in the mood for them. All these flowers . . . I find it sinister. I've become allergic to flowers. And the vases I had, I've thrown them all out.

Anne Except this one.

Madeleine I must have missed it.

8

Anne I'll put it here. Or if you prefer, I'll take it away. Up to you, Mum.

Madeleine shrugs her shoulders. Élise has put the shopping bags on the kitchen table.

Have you been shopping? You should have told me. I could have come with you.

Madeleine You were asleep. I wasn't going to wake you up. Anyway, I had Élise . . . You don't need a regiment to do a bit of shopping.

Élise Especially as you had more important things to do, if I understood correctly . . .

Anne What makes you say that?

Élise's mobile rings.

Élise Ah. I have to take this. Sorry. I'll be back.

She answers as she's heading for the door. She speaks into the phone.

I asked you not to call me any more . . . No!

She exits.

Anne What's the matter with her?

Madeleine I don't know. They never stop quarrelling on the phone . . . All morning, same performance.

Anne With Paul?

Madeleine The new one.

Anne Yes, that's right. He's called Paul.

Madeleine Are you sure? Maybe . . . I can never manage to keep up with all her dramas . . . What about you? How are you getting on? You went to bed late last night, didn't you?

Anne There are so many papers to sort out.

Madeleine I told you.

Anne Yes.

Madeleine I got up about three o'clock. Because of the storm. The light in the office was still on.

Anne Yes. I worked quite late.

Madeleine I don't understand why you insist on doing this.

Anne You know very well. His editor asked me to. But if you think it's a bad idea, nothing's forcing you to agree . . .

André Old papers.

Anne Sorry?

André Notes. Old papers. What's the appeal?

Anne They'd like to bring out an edition of all your unfinished pieces . . . Diaries . . . sketches . . . poems . . . Everything you didn't publish.

André raises his eyes to heaven. Clearly, he doesn't like the idea. Anne speaks to her mother, as she helps her to unpack the shopping.

They think it's a good way to get into his work. To understand it.

André There's nothing to understand. People who try to understand things are morons.

Anne (*to her mother*) His editor's very keen on this. Thinks of it as an *hommage*. But if you're against it, all you have to do is refuse.

Madeleine I don't know. Seems to me it's a bit like digging up a corpse. Don't you think? Not to mention the fact you'll never manage it in one weekend.

Anne I know.

Madeleine (*as if addressing a problem*) You'll have to come back.

Anne Yes, of course. Is that what's upsetting you?

Madeleine No. Except I was wondering . . . What would *he* have wanted? Would he have liked people rummaging around in his papers?

They look at each other. Pause. A break.

André What did you buy?

Madeleine What?

André In your shopping bag? You've just come back from the shops, haven't you? What did you buy?

Madeleine Mushrooms.

André Ah . . . Wonderful. For lunch?

Madeleine (*as if stating the obvious*) Yes.

André Show me.

Madeleine shows them to him.

Oh . . . Perfect. (*To his daughter.*) You'll see. For years we didn't eat them. We preferred meat. I don't know what we were thinking. But now . . . she's become a terrific mushroom cook. A real scorcher! What are the ingredients? Tell us again.

Madeleine Nothing worth saying . . .

André Nothing worth saying! Tell us all the same.

Madeleine A bit of parsley . . .

André (*to his daughter, his eyes shining*) A bit of parsley . . .

Madeleine An onion.

André (*to his daughter*) An onion. Yes, yes, that's it . . . Just an onion, cut in very thin slices, like that. Marvellous. One good onion.

Madeleine Salt and pepper . . .

André Salt and pepper, obviously!

Madeleine And that's it.

André And that's it. You see? (*To Madeleine.*) No chives?

Madeleine Oh, yes. Of course!

André (*to his daughter*) Ah, chives! Mustn't forget the chives! Green, red and yellow. All the colours. In an omelette. An omelette . . . Mmm . . . That's her specialty. My little scorcher.

Madeleine Stop calling me that.

André When are we eating?

Anne It's only eleven o'clock, Dad.

André (*clearly disappointed*) Is it? Is that all?

Madeleine Yes.

Anne Are you hungry already?

André Yes. Maybe. Aren't I?

Anne It's still a bit early.

André It's this talk about mushrooms . . . Eleven o'clock? Is that all?

Anne Yes.

André But on what day?

Anne (*kindly*) Today, Dad.

André Ah.

He seems lost and annoyed. He takes a few steps into the room, then stops.

I thought it was a different day. Isn't it? Unless . . .

He seems, suddenly, to have lost the thread. Madeleine continues to unpack her purchases.

Madeleine We'll sit down at the table in about an hour . . .

Anne Reading his diaries, I noticed he talked a lot about you.

Madeleine Are you surprised? Given we spent half a century together.

Anne I know. I was talking to Élise about that yesterday . . . It marked us in some ways, both of us.

Madeleine What?

Anne The fact you stayed together all that time. It's not very common, if you think about it. The ability to love one another to the end.

Madeleine How's it going with Pierre?

Anne moves closer to the kitchen table.

Anne Would you like me to chop them?

Madeleine No, no. Leave them. I'll do it.

Brief pause.

Are things not going well?

Anne It's complicated. Especially with Emma, it's really not easy.

Madeleine Why?

Anne She's supposed to take her exams this year. But she's doing nothing. She's skipping all her courses. She . . . Well, she's behaving very strangely.

Madeleine It'll calm down. Give her time.

Anne shrugs her shoulders. She doesn't look convinced.

Anne I remember. He loved these.

Madeleine What?

Anne Mushrooms.

Madeleine (*to her daughter*) There was a time, he even used to go and pick them. Remember?

Anne Did he?

Madeleine (*to her daughter*) Don't you remember? He always used to walk a lot. Said it helped him think.

André's listening to what they're saying and trying to remember.

When he got back, he'd go straight to his study and write . . . His best ideas came to him while he was walking.

André Yes.

Madeleine When we left Paris and settled in here, he took it into his head to go and pick mushrooms . . . He did that for a year or two. It used to make me laugh. He'd put on his hat and all the gear . . . I used to make fun of him . . . And then, suddenly, he stopped.

André Who are you talking about?

Anne (*as if André hadn't spoken*) Why?

Madeleine The really good mushrooms, you'd find them along the river. Not far from Saint-Pierre. It's a dangerous path. Very slippery. And one day, we heard about someone who'd disappeared just like that. Armanet! Does that name mean anything to you?

Anne No.

Madeleine Yes, it does. Madame Armanet's husband. They never found out what happened to him, he never came back. Everybody thought he'd slipped and fallen in the river. So your father, who was never the most courageous man . . . His obsession was always his work. Write, write, write . . . The rest was . . .

Anne I know.

Madeleine So, the mushrooms, you can imagine! He kept on going for walks, but nowhere near the river.

André But who, who is it you're talking about?

Madeleine Armanet.

André frowns, as if the name evokes some confused memory.

André Ah.

Anne Last night, I came across . . . You were saying he never stopped writing. But I was surprised to see that towards the end, he was still writing a lot . . .

Madeleine Well!

Anne Recently . . . just seeing his handwriting . . . it's been . . . I don't know . . .

She breaks off, overcome with emotion.

Madeleine What's the matter?

Anne Nothing. It's . . .

Madeleine What's the matter with you?

Anne Nothing. I said. It's the onions.

Madeleine comes over to her daughter and takes her in her arms.

15

Madeleine Come on, come on . . .

They stay like that, in each other's arms, not speaking, as can happen between a mother and a daughter, without quite knowing why, when the subject is painful.

André (*not looking at the two women behind him*) Yes, he used to live other side of the hill. Armanet, I mean. We knew his wife better. Friend of your mother's. Some people thought he'd found some poisonous mushrooms. There are plenty of them round here. They can kill you . . . But then they would have found the body . . . The path along the river seemed more likely . . . Except, years later, I bumped into him in Paris in a station. Can you believe it? I'm almost sure it was him. I was staggered. I couldn't get over it. I went over to him. And I said to him: 'Armanet? Is that you?' And then, I saw his face distorted with terror. Terror. Colossal. Gigantic. 'You must be mistaken . . .' That's what he said to me. Then he ran for it, fast. You think people are dead, but it's not always the case . . . You know what I mean? He was with a woman . . . But I never told anybody. I kept it to myself. Naturally. It's everyone's right to take their secrets with them, don't you agree?

He turns towards the two women and sees that they are in each other's arms.

What's the matter with her?

The two women move apart. Everything is as if they've heard nothing of the story he's just told them. Everything's as if he weren't there at all.

Madeleine Come on.

Anne Yes.

Madeleine All right?

Anne (*to her mother*) Yes. Yes. I'm sorry. Forgive me.

André What's the matter with her?

Anne smiles broadly to dispel this attack of sadness.

Anne I ought to be braver.

Madeleine Not at all. It's quite normal. Nothing to worry about.

Anne It's all been so sudden.

Madeleine I know. Come on.

Anne Yes. Yes. Sorry. Right. I should get back to it. I . . . You'll call me if you need me?

Madeleine All right.

Anne Unless I can help you . . . You want me to do the onions?

Madeleine (*smiling*) What, and make yourself cry again? No, no. Off you go. Go and work. I'll call you when it's ready.

Anne All right. See you soon . . .

She goes out. Madeleine begins to peel the mushrooms.

Madeleine I know you've always thought she was hard. But, believe me, things aren't easy for her at the moment.

Pause.

Élise tells me she's in the middle of separating from Pierre. I'm not supposed to know.

Pause.

She found out he was seeing another woman. Younger, of course . . . For several months. So, inevitably . . . And with everything that's going on here, it hasn't been easy for her . . .

Pause.

Are you hungry?

André doesn't answer.

It won't be long.

He goes over to the window and looks into the distance, as at the beginning.

What are you looking at?

Pause. No answer.

Is it because of the storm? We need to check the vegetable garden . . . The amount that came down last night. I hope there hasn't been too much damage.

Pause. She suddenly stops what she's doing, troubled by a thought.

Who's going to look after it now, the vegetable garden?

Pause.

André? Are you listening to me? The vegetable garden . . . Who's going to look after it?

Pause. He turns towards her.

What's the matter?

André I can't understand why you ask her to come and see us . . .

Madeleine Who? Anne? I didn't ask her. She wanted to spend the weekend here.

André Why?

Madeleine Why do you think? To help you. Not to leave you on your own.

André Help me? Help me do what? I don't need anything. No, I don't like it. This business of interfering in other people's lives. And it's both of them . . .

He glances out of the window.

Look, the other one's out there . . . Still on the phone . . .

Madeleine They mean well . . .

André Mean well? You know what Anne just said to me? She's invited some estate agent to drop by! She made an appointment . . . And he's supposed to come tomorrow. Here! D'you realise? The least you can say is they're not wasting any time. And the excuse is they want to help me!

Pause.

You know what I am, I'm an old plant in an old pot. You can't uproot me. I'll manage very well by myself.

Madeleine You? Manage by yourself? You can't even make yourself a meal.

André I'll manage.

Madeleine smiles.

What? What's so funny?

Madeleine Nothing. I'm just thinking about you in the kitchen . . .

André I don't deny it, I've never had the knack for all that . . . for anything concrete.

Madeleine After all these years . . .

André Yes, I know. I know.

Madeleine I wonder what would have become of you without me.

André It's true. I can see you now, getting the lunch ready . . . Over there.

He indicates the kitchen, where indeed Madeleine is.

André Organising our lives . . . Organising everything . . .
All these years . . . It's true. I can see you. So present. So
strong . . . All the same! That's not a reason for the way
they've come in to land. Wanting to change everything
without consulting me! I mean, d'you realise? An estate
agent! What are they trying to do? Sell the house, is that
it? On the pretext that to do the shopping you have to get
in the car? What about me? What's to become of me in
all this? Where am I supposed to go?

Madeleine You'll have to talk to them about it.

André No point. Things are very clear. I am not leaving
this house. Out of the question! I shan't move from here!

Élise comes in.

Élise (*referring to her phone call*) I'm really sorry, forgive
me, I had to take it. (*To her father.*) Are you all right?

She strokes his face.

What's the matter? You don't seem to be in a very good
mood . . .

Madeleine Have you ever seen your father in a good
mood?

*Élise smiles; without, however, having heard what her
mother's just said.*

Élise What's the matter, little daddy?

André Nothing. It's just . . .

Élise What?

André Nothing. Nothing. Who were you talking to?
I saw you through the window. Were you on the phone?

Élise Yes. I was talking to Paul.

André Paul?

Élise My lover.

André The one who runs the driving school?

Élise No, that's Daniel.

André Oh?

Madeleine passes in front of them on her way to the front door.

Élise It's Daniel who works at the driving school. But things are . . .

André (*to Madeleine*) Are you going out?

Madeleine I'll be back.

André (*anxiously*) Where are you going?

Madeleine To look for some chives . . .

André Now?

Madeleine Yes. In the vegetable garden. I'll be back. Don't make that face, I'll only be a minute . . .

André seems anxious about the fact she's leaving. She goes out. He moves towards the door, like a child whose mother is leaving.

Élise Anyway, I don't live with him any more. Daniel.

André Oh?

Élise No, it started getting impossible.

André She's gone down to the garden.

Élise Things weren't working between us. I mean . . .

André Erm . . .

Élise Things were starting to get contentious and . . .

André She'll be back soon. Don't worry.

Élise Sorry?

André Mm?

Élise Who are you talking about?

André Your mother. She'll be back soon.

Élise Dad . . .

André What?

Élise reaches out for her father with a tender gesture. As if she were convinced her mother wasn't coming back and that he's comforting himself with illusions.

She's gone out to look for . . . But she's coming back. With the chives. From the vegetable garden. She always puts chives in the mushrooms. All three colours. And onions. She mixes them all up. Then she . . . She has her own recipe. No, no, she's just stepped into the garden . . . For . . . So don't worry. Yes, for . . .

Élise Dad . . .

André What?

Élise I was talking to you about Paul.

André Who?

Élise Paul, not Daniel, he was before. I don't live with him any more.

André Just as you like.

He's only listening to Élise with half an ear, still concerned about Madeleine's absence.

Élise I met a man I really love, his name is Paul.

André I see.

Élise And the good news is, I'm going to be able to introduce him to you! He's just told me he's going to come down here!

André Who?

Élise Paul! He had meetings this weekend, but he finally decided to cancel them.

André Oh, did he?

Élise Yes! He wanted to be with me. He cares about me, you see. For once, I think I've landed on somebody kind . . . He doesn't want to leave me on my own. Considering the situation.

André frowns. For the first time, he seems to be listening to what she's saying. What situation is she referring to? Élise realises he's somewhat lost.

The situation, Dad . . . I've explained it to him. He couldn't come to the funeral on Saturday. He was very sorry. Really. He would have loved to have been there. With us. But he had some very important meetings. Some bit of his contract had to be settled just at that moment. Anyway, he had no choice. But you'll see him soon. Because he's coming to see us. That's good news, isn't it?

André But . . .

Élise Isn't it?

Pause. André is trying to understand.

You know, I'm really looking forward to introducing him to you. And he is too, he's really happy he's going to meet you. I've told him a lot about you. He's the one who put me in touch with the Blue House.

André The Blue House?

Élise Yes.

André What's that?

Madeleine comes back with the chives.

Ah, there you are!

Madeleine Where else did you expect me to be?

André What's this business about the Blue House?

Élise Mm?

André This business . . . What is it?

Élise turns towards Madeleine, a little embarrassed, and not knowing what to say.

Madeleine What?

André The Blue House?

Madeleine shrugs her shoulders. She doesn't know what he's talking about.

I'm beginning to think you're hiding something from me. I don't like that.

Madeleine No, we're not! Whatever will you think of next? By the way, I forgot to tell you. In the market, I bumped into someone you used to know.

André Who?

Madeleine This morning. Mrs Scharz? Mrs Schwart? Does that mean anything to you?

André Mrs who?

Madeleine Schartwz. Or something like that.

André Never heard of her.

Élise Look, give me the chives, I'll rinse them . . .

Madeleine Mrs Schwartz or . . . She came up to me in the street to talk about you. She said you know each other very well . . . that you'd known each other years ago . . . She was with her son . . . They're staying round here for a few days . . . She wanted to know how you were . . .

André But I don't even know who you're talking about!

Madeleine I'm talking about your friend . . .

André What friend?

Madeleine Mrs Schartz?

André shrugs his shoulders.

Élise Was that the woman you were talking to just now? In the market? Brown hair?

Madeleine Yes.

Élise She was strange. Don't you think?

Madeleine She wanted to come and say hello to you . . .

André Me?

Madeleine Yes. According to what she told me, you knew each other when you were children. Then, in Paris, you were part of the same little group. That was her expression. 'The same little group.' That's why . . .

André Don't tell me you suggested she come round . . .

Madeleine I thought you'd be pleased.

André (*appalled*) What?

Madeleine I suggested she come for tea.

André Are you joking? When?

Madeleine Today.

André You mean she's going to come here?

Madeleine Is that a problem for you?

André (*becoming agitated*) But I don't even know who this woman is. You're saying a name I don't recognise . . . A German name . . . No. No. I don't know her. All this

25

has nothing to do with me. All these stories. Nothing, d'you understand? We're not going to go through all that again!

Madeleine What are you talking about?

André You have to cancel it. Did you give her the address?

Madeleine She knew it. I told you, she spoke about you as if at one time you'd been really close. Mrs Schwartz? I even wondered if you'd . . . well, you know what I mean.

André (*racked with misery*) She's lying. I don't know who this woman is. Or what she's looking for . . .

Madeleine I'm sure when you see her, you'll recognise her.

André No! No! No!

Madeleine But why are you getting yourself in this state?

André (*agitated*) All you have to do is tell her I'm not here. That I've left.

Madeleine But . . .

André Tell her she's come too late. I'm not here. Not to be seen. Sick, whatever you like.

Madeleine If that's what you want . . . I thought you'd be pleased, that's all.

André No.

Madeleine I mean, if an old friend of mine were to surface, I'd be happy to have a cup of tea with her!

André Well, I wouldn't.

Madeleine Find out what had become of her . . .

André (*vehemently*) I said *no*. Understand?

Madeleine All right. No need to take that tone.

André takes refuge in a corner of the room. Pause. Uncomfortable atmosphere. Élise takes a step towards him.

Élise Dad . . .

André Why do you all have to dredge up my past like this? What are you looking for? I haven't committed a crime, as far as I know.

Madeleine No one's said you had.

André Well, then? Leave me in peace! And the other one's rummaging through my papers . . .

Madeleine That's quite normal. In these circumstances, that's what people do.

André In what circumstances?

Madeleine Mm?

André In what circumstances? What are you talking about?

Élise (*gently*) You know very well.

Pause. He's trying to understand. Why is she talking to him as if he were dead?

Anyway, I wonder who could have sent these flowers . . .

Madeleine What's it matter?

Élise searches through the bouquet.

Élise The card must have fallen out.

Madeleine And I did say . . . No flowers . . . But no, nobody was listening. It's always the same.

Élise Anyway, they smell nice.

Madeleine He would have hated this.

André Who?

Madeleine (*as if he hadn't spoken*) All these flowers . . . He would have found it ridiculous. And in the street . . . Did you see? When I was out . . . All these people coming up and speaking to me . . .

Élise It's natural. People admired him a lot.

Madeleine Maybe. But this thing of endlessly talking to me about him. It's even more irritating than the flowers . . .

Élise All the same, with this woman, you were saying she . . .

Madeleine Yes, well, she's different. I don't know. There was something about her. Don't you think?

Élise shrugs her shoulders.

Mrs Scwartz . . . Why did you say you thought she was strange?

Élise Just an impression. But I didn't speak to her. I was on the phone with Paul. I wasn't listening to what you were saying to each other.

Madeleine I think she knew him very well.

André No . . .

Madeleine When he was young. At the time of his first successes. I'm looking forward to talking to her about it. It's quite simple.

André No.

Madeleine To be able to talk to someone who knew him well.

Élise I understand.

André (*panicking*) But I don't understand. *At all.* I don't understand any of it!

They stop and look at him, as if sizing up his presence for the first time.

(*His voice choked.*) I'm here.

Hiatus. It almost seems as if they're about to speak to him. But suddenly, they no longer see him. It's as if a mirage has cleared. They return to what they were doing.

Madeleine Right, well I'm going to get lunch ready.

Élise Sure I can't help you?

Madeleine No, no, I'll deal with it.

She goes into the kitchen.

Élise Just as you like.

André I'm here!

Madeleine If the weather holds, we could try and eat outside.

Élise Good idea . . .

André I . . . I . . . There, there's my chair. I can still sit in it. And there are the flowers . . . I can still smell them. There's the window. The door. The lamp. And me. I'm here. I . . . Look at me . . .

No reaction.

Madeleine . . .

She doesn't seem to see him. Seized with fear, he turns towards Élise, who has sat down in his chair and now absently opens a book.

I'm still here . . . I'm . . . You can see! I . . . I'm here.
Among you. I'm here. I . . . Aren't I? Look. I'm still here.
I am. Can you hear me? I'm here . . .

But his words seem to disappear into the void.
Despair. Pause.

Blackout.

Two

The same room, a little later. Madeleine and Mrs Schwartz are having tea. The latter might appear to be younger than Madeleine. In any case, she doesn't correspond physically to the description of 'childhood friend'. Élise is also there. At the start, she's playing with her mobile, as if this conversation doesn't really interest her. In one corner a Man can be seen, whose presence is not explained. Everyone behaves as if he isn't there; in the same way, he pays no attention to what's going on in the room. He's busy with some solitary activity: sharpening knives, for example.

Woman He was an exceptional man. I've often thought about him, through all these years. I read his books, which I found shattering, and every time I could see again the young man I'd known. I admired him very much, you know . . . And then I run into you today, I heard someone say your name in the market and I said to myself, 'That's her,' and came over to you with no clear idea of what I might say to you. You were together and . . .

Pause.

You have two daughters, is that right?

Madeleine Yes. Anne and Élise. And . . . what about you?

Woman A son.

Madeleine Oh?

Woman You saw him just now.

Madeleine Oh, yes. Yes.

Woman A wonderful boy. I brought him up on my own. Well, you know . . .

Élise looks up from her mobile. Pause.

Madeleine Not long ago, he showed me an article he'd cut out of the newspaper. A story which had caught his interest . . . Maybe you heard about it? It happened about three years ago . . . The story of an elderly couple who'd booked a suite at a big hotel in Paris . . . The Lutetia, I believe. Does that ring a bell?

Woman I don't know.

Madeleine It was the hotel where they'd got married decades earlier. That evening they had dinner in the big restaurant and went to bed asking not to be disturbed. The next day when the maid finally went into their room, she found them stretched out on the bed. Fully clothed. Both of them. They'd taken something. The newspaper said it was some kind of mushroom . . . Anyway, they were no longer breathing.

Woman Do you mean they'd committed suicide?

Madeleine One of them was already ill. And they were quite old. They knew there was nothing very interesting in store for them. Retirement homes, hospitals, all that . . . They didn't want that. And they didn't want to be a burden on their children. So, you see . . . They preferred to leave with dignity. In each other's arms.

Woman Creepy.

Madeleine You think so? At the time, when he made me read the article, that's how I reacted. But today I'm wondering if . . .

Brief pause.

Élise If what?

Madeleine How can I put it? I think his greatest fear was that I might die before he did . . . He wouldn't have been able to bear that. To find himself completely on his own. He wouldn't have been capable of managing without me. I don't say that to give myself any particular importance. It's just the way it was. He wasn't able to adjust to the simplest things in life. Anything concrete. He used to talk about it sometimes. It would have been a nightmare for him. A real nightmare.

Woman So in some ways . . .

Madeleine Yes. It's my only consolation. He made me promise to outlive him. A bit stupid. Not to go before him. And I'm not the kind of person who doesn't keep her promises.

Pause. She pulls herself together.

I'm sorry. I don't know why I'm burdening you with all this! Instead, why don't you tell me . . . You, I mean! I still haven't worked out when you got to know one another . . . You seem so much younger than him . . .

Anne comes in.

Ah, here she is . . . This is my other daughter . . .

Anne comes over and shakes hands.

Anne Hello.

Madeleine Anne, Mrs Schwarz. A childhood friend of your father's.

Anne It's a pleasure.

Woman Not exactly a childhood friend . . . We came from the same part of the world, so, when I went to study in Paris, we had a lot of mutual friends. Georges, in particular.

Anne Georges?

Woman I won't deny we had a relationship, the two of us. For many years.

Madeleine You what?

Anne You had a relationship with . . .

Woman Yes.

Brief pause. Then she clarifies what she's said.

With Georges. André's friend.

Madeleine Ah.

Woman Georges Dulon. Name doesn't mean anything? I was always around . . . I was fascinated by them. They'd started up this little literary magazine . . . But all that's so long ago. A century ago.

Pause.

Madeleine (*to her daughters*) When I met your father, he didn't tell me anything about his life. Sometimes you really had to nag him to get him to answer questions.

Anne I know.

Madeleine He was a very secretive man.

Pause.

(*To Anne.*) Would you like a cup of tea? Come and sit with us.

Anne No, thanks. I'd better get back.

Madeleine My daughter's trying to sort through André's papers.

Woman Oh, yes?

Madeleine Yes. He kept a kind of private diary, which he never published. And his editor, who knew about

34

the existence of these diaries, asked her if she could find them. That's why she's here.

Anne It's not the only reason.

Madeleine Isn't it?

Élise You know very well, Mum, we came to be with you.

Madeleine Perhaps you did . . .

Pause.

Woman And have you read these diaries?

Anne I've just started. They're not always very legible . . .

Woman I imagine that must be quite unsettling. Isn't it? The image you construct of someone is bound to be invented. And suddenly you find out . . . the truth. And there's always something scandalous about the truth. Don't you think?

Pause. Uncomfortably, Madeleine holds out the teapot in the Woman's direction.

Madeleine Would you . . .?

Woman Thank you. Delicious tea.

Madeleine Thanks. (*To Anne.*) Is he still asleep?

Anne No. I think I heard him.

Madeleine Could you go and check? Tell him his friend has arrived.

Élise Never mind. I'll go.

Anne No, no. I'll take care of it.

Anne goes out.

Madeleine He has a siesta, every day at the same time.

Woman Oh?

Madeleine Yes. He's done it for years. I'm sorry. I thought he'd have woken up a bit earlier.

Woman It's all right. I'm not in any hurry . . .

Pause.

Madeleine As I told you, he has moments of complete alertness. Brilliant insights. Epiphanies. And then other moments of confusion and incoherence . . . of fog . . . But I think he'd be happy to be able to talk to you about that time of his life . . . To recall the past.

Élise Anyway, when we told him we'd run into you this morning, he seemed happy. I mean, at the idea of seeing you again . . . Didn't he?

Woman Me too! To me, he's the greatest writer of his generation. I admired him so much.

Pause.

(*To Élise.*) My brother had this kind of . . . He also had problems with his memory. But they didn't find out about it until very late on. I must say, his wife did everything she could to stop people realising.

Madeleine Oh, yes?

Woman (*to Élise*) She was very good at it. She would answer for him, always kept ahead of him in the conversation, took possession of the field . . . So well, no one really grasped the situation. It was only when she disappeared that we realised how ill he was.

Élise So what did you do?

Woman We had to put him in a nursing home. It was very painful.

Élise I'm sure.

Woman All the more so because it happened very suddenly. His wife was so . . . strong. Younger than him. No one was expecting her to go first . . . And then one morning she got up, went to do some gardening and dropped dead. Quite simply.

Madeleine (*apparently concerned*) Doing some gardening? Do you mean . . . in the vegetable garden?

No one answers. The Woman rests her hand on Élise's forearm, as if she wanted to support her.

Woman Don't worry. I'm sure everything will be all right.

Élise Let's hope so.

André appears, followed by Anne. He sees Mrs Schwartz.

Élise Ah! You're awake!

André No.

Élise Come and have some tea with us! We've been waiting for you.

André What . . . ?

The Woman gets up.

Woman André! How are you?

André Me?

Woman It's been such a long time . . .

He looks questioningly at his wife. Who is this woman?

Madeleine I told you I ran into your friend this morning.

André Did you?

Madeleine In the market.

André (*as if he's remembered*) Oh, yes!

Madeleine Yes! And I invited her to come to the house for tea. Mrs Scartzw. You remember?

Woman How wonderful to see you again! I've often thought about you, you know . . .

André That's nice. But . . .

Woman After all these years . . .

André Yes, yes. Right. Is that right? Yes, yes. Yes, that's right. That is right, isn't it? That's right. Right. That's right. Yes, yes, yes.

Madeleine (*somewhat embarrassed*) Mrs Scatrtz is passing through the area. I said to myself, you'd be happy to see one another.

She turns towards the Woman.

As I understand it, you were friends when he was starting out?

Woman Yes. There was a whole little group of us . . . As I was telling you, André and Georges were inseparable. He'd just published his first novel. Isn't that right? He was already famous. Everyone admired him. So . . . But you couldn't say we were especially intimate.

Madeleine No? I thought you said . . .

Woman No. Later, yes, we did have a, let's say, special relationship.

Anne Special?

Woman Yes. That's the right word, I think. Isn't it?

André I don't know.

Woman I remember it as if it were yesterday. We all went on holiday and stayed at a friend's house . . . Laurent. Remember?

André Laurent?

Woman Yes, I . . .

André Laurent Marignan?

Woman Yes! That's right. I'd forgotten his surname.

André It was Marignan.

Woman Yes!

André Charming boy. His father had made some sort of dubious fortune . . .

Woman I remember! You're absolutely right!

Élise (*to her sister*) You see, he remembers.

André Arms dealer or something . . . wasn't he?

Woman Mm? I . . . I don't know.

André Drug trafficker.

Woman I . . . Really?

André Or pig-breeder?

Woman I thought he was a journalist.

André That's right.

Woman Anyway, they had this house . . . By the water, in Corsica . . . and we went down there.

André Yes, yes. I remember the sea. It was blue. And flat.

Woman (*to the daughters*) Everyone spent the day on the beach, but not him, he stayed in the house, working. He was writing. He never stopped writing. One day I got back from the beach ahead of the others, and inadvertently went into the library where he'd got into the habit of withdrawing to work. And I saw he was crying. I'll remember it my whole life. He was crying. How can

I explain? I'd never seen anyone crying like that . . . He was like an utterly desperate child and I was shattered. I didn't know what to do. I was so impressed by the intensity of his grief. So I went to him and, without even thinking about it, I kissed him.

Madeleine You . . .

Woman I kissed him and we made love. Without speaking a single word.

Madeleine knocks over her cup.

From then on, yes, I think you could say we had a powerful relationship. He said I was the only one who knew how to console him.

Madeleine is pretending to pick up her cup. She straightens out the tea-tray and takes it into the kitchen, watched uneasily by her daughters.

It lasted many years. Even after he got married, I think I can now tell you . . . After a certain amount of time, this kind of detail is not so important any more. Don't you think? He had me read what he wrote. Always. I was at his side. He claimed he needed my opinion to be able to continue to write, that I was *the* woman in his life. The woman in his life . . . He never stopped saying it. But I think he only said it out of kindness.

Anne But who are you talking about?

Woman Mm?

Anne Who are you talking about?

Woman Georges! Georges Dulon.

Anne Oh . . . You . . .

Woman André's friend. Do you remember him? You started that literary magazine together . . .

Anne Do you remember Georges Dulon?

André Who?

Woman Sadly, he never had a career like yours. He died in a car accident. A real disaster.

André I'm sorry, I . . . I think you're making a mistake . . . I don't know a . . . Who you were talking about . . . Who exactly were we talking about?

Woman Who do you think?

Brief pause.

For years I asked him to acknowledge his son, but he was never very courageous about that. He was married. He had children. Classic situation, really . . .

Madeleine (*very upset*) I don't understand anything about this story.

Woman He always used to say: 'You'll sort it out when I'm dead . . .' That was his big expression. 'You'll always be able to claim your share, when I'm dead . . .'

Madeleine Who said that?

Woman So I said nothing. I waited. And I brought him up all on my own. But one day these sorts of stories have to be resolved, don't you agree? That a man refuses to acknowledge his son doesn't alter the fact that this son does have a father. I say that with no inheritance considerations, so that everything between us can be out in the open.

Madeleine (*agitated*) But *who* is she talking about? André . . .

Élise Dad!

André Fragments. False starts. Nothing much else.

Élise What?

André You believe in your own life. You lean back on it. The way you would lean back on a really solid rock. But what's the weight of it today? There's no grip. That's the problem.

Anne What's he saying?

André I had a life. I don't deny it. But in the end, what's left? A few faces? A few names lost in the fog? Here and there . . . Not much more. May as well forget everything.

Pause. Unease. Madeleine leaves the cups, leaves the kitchen, and, watched anxiously by André, silently disappears towards the bedrooms, as if wounded by what she's just learned. André remains in suspense: why has she left the room? What's happened? He takes a step in her direction.

Where are you going?

Élise Dad . . . I'm finding this conversation a bit incoherent . . .

Anne (*ironically*) You think so? It's absolutely all over the place.

Élise I . . . It seems to me we're talking about something different from where we started out.

André Why did she leave like that? Did I say something?

Anne Who?

André Your mother . . .

The women look at each other. Why is he still talking about her?

Élise Listen, I'd like you to try to understand why we're taking this step . . .

André Understand what?

Élise Mrs Scharzt –

André (*interrupting her*) Yes, I know. I know. You already told me.

Élise No, you don't know.

Woman Don't worry. It's normal for him to react like this . . .

Élise (*to Mrs Schwartz, as if trying to apologise for the situation*) I'm really sorry.

Woman I'm saying. It takes time for everyone to adapt to a new situation.

Élise The way it happened, it was so sudden.

Woman I know.

Élise We weren't prepared. He wasn't. Neither were we.

Woman I understand.

Élise She was so full of energy . . . So alive!

André turns to Élise. What is she talking about?

Anne I've known for years my mobile would ring one day and I'd be told this sort of news. Bad news. I was used to the idea. But strangely, I never expected this.

Élise I didn't either. And it has to be said, she was younger than him. She was so strong. So present.

Anne Nothing to be done. You just have to adapt to the situation. However painful it is, that goes without saying.

She speaks now to her father.

That's the reason, Dad . . .

Pause.

Élise Dad . . .

André What?

Élise Mrs Armanet was telling us that her brother . . .

She turns towards the Woman.

That's right, isn't it?

Woman Yes, my brother . . . lost his wife, as well, a couple of years ago. They were very close . . .

Élise And when she . . . When she'd gone . . .

Woman Yes. We had to find another arrangement.

Anne So he wouldn't be completely on his own.

Woman Quite.

Élise And that's why you heard us talking about the Blue House . . .

Woman Exactly. He moved in there, and really it was . . . I mean, it's very well organised. It was perfect. Very pleasant and . . . he had a little room with a view of the park.

Élise Oh? Hear that, Dad, there's a park.

Woman He could go for a walk every day. With the other residents. Or on his own, if he felt like it.

Anne And I saw there was a lake as well, isn't there?

Woman Yes, there's a lake. With ducks. In fact, whenever I went to see him, he was always sitting on the same bench, facing the lake, feeding the ducks with little bits of bread. He loved doing that. That's what they told me over there. Right up to the end, he was feeding the ducks.

Pause. André goes over to the door through which Madeleine left. He opens it. He stops. Where is she? He turns towards his daughters.

44

Anne You know, we've thought a lot about this and if we talk to you about it, it's because we honestly think it's the best solution. But we wanted Mrs Armanet to come and talk to you about it herself.

Woman It'll suit you very well, André. Believe me.

Anne Yes, you'll be very happy there.

Élise Anne is right. Everything'll be fine . . .

André But in the end they fly away.

Élise Sorry?

André The ducks. In the end they do fly away. And then it's the vultures' turn. You see them wheeling above your head.

Anne What are you . . . ?

André And the vultures feast in broad daylight.

Anne doesn't know what to say to this. He moves forward towards the bouquet of flowers, which is still in the middle of the room. He looks for something among the flowers. A card?

Élise What are you doing, Dad? What are you looking for?

André Some sense!

Anne Dad . . .

André We will break through the darkness with daylight. We will find the door. Because there must be one, mustn't there? There must be some sense to all this! Isn't there?

The Man, in his corner, starts to laugh, still sharpening his knives.

If not, what is my position? What is my position here? What is my position? My position! What is my position

45

here? My position. Here. What is it? My position . . .
what is it?

*Suddenly, he turns towards his daughters. Full of
emotion, as if he were now talking about his wife and
indicating the door through which she left.*

Where is she?

Blackout.

Three

The following morning. Élise is with the Man.

Élise Are you still angry with me?

The Man doesn't answer.

Are you still annoyed?

Man No, no.

Élise Anyway, I'm really glad you're here.

Man Are you?

Élise Yes, really. That you were able to meet him. It was important for me that you came out here. That you're with me.

Man What are you talking about? Everything's as it should be.

Élise Would you like another coffee?

The Man shakes his head.

When do you have to be back in Paris? Noon, is that right? We'll have to leave in an hour if you don't want to be late.

Man Fine. But you could always stay . . .

Élise No. I want to be with you.

She smiles at him.

I'd just like to drop by the cemetery on our way. If that doesn't inconvenience you.

Man No.

Élise Just to drop by. It won't take much time.

Man Of course. No problem.

Élise To be honest, I was a bit scared about how he was going to react.

Man Your father?

Élise Yes. It's a long time since I've seen him, you know. Quite a few weeks . . . I hadn't realised things had . . . I mean . . . Yesterday, for example, I made the mistake of inviting a family friend for tea. He didn't even recognise her.

Man Yes, you told me.

Élise It was so strange. I could see it in his eyes. He was lost . . . Everything was mixed up in his head . . . That's why I was a bit nervous about how he would react to you.

Man But in the end, as you saw, everything went well.

Élise Yes. Very well. He was charming. Don't you think? You can't imagine the kind of man he was . . . He had a very special kind of strength . . . Everyone admired him. But basically, he owed most of what he'd achieved to my mother. She was always there. Backing him up . . . Her going was enough for everything to collapse. I mean, for him to completely lose his bearings . . .

Man Come on . . .

Élise And my sister, what did you think of her?

Man Very nice.

Élise No, seriously . . . Tell me . . .

The Man smiles.

You see what I mean?

The Man nods.

She's always been like that. So serious . . . When I was little, I was jealous of her.

Man You?

Élise I had terrible complexes, because I wasn't as . . . How can I describe it? I wasn't like them. I was interested in other things. Less important things, no doubt. She, she wanted to be a writer. That's what she wanted to do with her life. Write. She was very ambitious. And then, in the end, she did nothing.

Man Why not?

Élise I don't know. Perhaps it was difficult to get past Dad. She's always had a complicated relationship with him. At the same time, she resented him. But I don't know what for.

Anne appears.

Anne Are you talking about me?

Élise Ah, you're up already?

Anne What were you just saying?

Élise Nothing. I was saying . . . I was explaining to Paul that you were always Dad's favourite.

Anne looks daggers at her.

Why are you looking at me like that? It's true, isn't it?

Anne Stop talking nonsense. Is he up?

Élise I don't know.

Anne Did you sleep well?

Man Very. Really . . . It's so calm, this house!

Anne Anybody want a coffee?

Man No, thanks.

Élise We've already had breakfast. And, you know, we don't have much time.

Anne What, are you planning to leave this morning?

Élise Yes. Paul has to be in Paris by noon. We'd like to have stayed longer. But . . .

Man Yes. It's an important meeting. I'm sorry.

Élise We thought we'd pass by the cemetery on our way. If you'd like to come with us . . . Or maybe you'd like us to drive you back to Paris? There's room in the car . . .

Anne What about him?

Élise What?

Anne Are you planning to leave him here on his own?

Pause.

Élise Why are you speaking to me in that tone?

Anne What tone?

Élise That reproachful tone . . . As if I was abandoning him . . .

Anne I didn't say that.

Élise You suggested it.

Anne Not at all.

Élise As if I felt no concern about the situation.

Anne And do you feel any concern?

Pause.

Élise I don't understand what you're . . . Of course I feel concerned! How can you imagine I'm not?

Pause. She controls herself.

I was just saying to Paul that it really unsettled me, seeing him like that yesterday.

Anne You speak as if you've only just become aware of his condition.

Élise I hadn't imagined it was so . . . advanced.

Anne I have to say it's a long time since you've been to see them.

Pause.

Élise In any case, Paul spoke to the woman who runs it on the phone . . .

Man Yes . . .

Élise And she suggests we go and visit the place next Thursday.

Anne Yes, you told me.

Élise Then why are you asking if I feel concerned?

Pause.

I'm sure he'll like the park. Since he's so fond of walking . . . Don't you think?

Suddenly, André appears.

Ah, Dad!

Anne Are you up already? Did you sleep well?

He doesn't answer.

Élise Come and sit down . . . I'll fix your croissants.

André Is it morning?

Anne Yes.

André Where's your mother?

Élise With strawberry jam, look . . . Come and sit down. Would you like something, Anne?

Anne No, I'll just have a coffee. Thanks.

André I haven't seen her this morning. Is she not here?

Anne No.

André Has she gone shopping?

Pause.

Or is she in her vegetable garden?

Élise Yes, I expect so.

André Ah.

He goes over to the window to try to see her.

She didn't wake me up this morning. I hate being the last up.

Élise Come on . . . Come and sit down.

André suddenly notices the Man.

You remember Paul?

André Ah . . . Yes. I . . . So? How's it going?

Man What?

André The driving school.

Man Sorry?

Élise No, Dad, you're getting confused . . . Paul doesn't work in a driving school. He's an estate agent.

André Oh, you . . . Are you the one? Is he the one? Is he?

Anne Élise planned to leave this morning. They would really have liked to stay a bit longer, but Paul has a work meeting, isn't that right?

Man Exactly. A viewing. It's Sunday, but it was the only day possible for my clients. I'm very sorry.

André You're an estate agent?

Man Yes.

André But . . . And my daughter told you to come?

Man (*uncertainly*) Yes.

Anne So, I was telling you, Élise has to go back, but you'll see her again on Thursday, isn't that it?

Élise Yes, Thursday. I'll be back and we'll spend the day together and . . . We'll go for a walk in a park.

Anne All right?

André But . . .

Anne Yes?

André This estate agent business . . .

Anne What?

André I don't want to sell the house.

Anne But nobody's said anything about selling the house, Dad.

André Yesterday, you told me . . .

Anne No, I didn't, Dad . . . Stop all that, please don't.

André But you told me . . .

Anne I never said that.

André I'm sorry, you told me . . .

Anne (*annoyed*) What?

Brief pause. He no longer knows the answer.

No one has any intention of selling the house. Why would you sell it?

Pause.

Élise Good. I'll go and pack my things.

André You've had breakfast already?

Élise Yes, thanks. I . . . I'll be back.

Anne (*to Élise*) Can I talk to you for a second?

Élise Mm? Yes. If you like . . .

Anne Just for a second. I'll be back.

They leave. Pause.

Man Anyway, it's a beautiful house. You won't have any trouble finding a purchaser if you do decide to sell . . . I mean . . . Beautiful proportions and a through light . . . It has something . . . Don't you think?

He takes a step towards André, who seems to be afraid of him.

Don't you agree with me? I'm sure you do. On this subject, at any rate.

André I . . . I don't know. Maybe.

Man You have no opinion on the matter?

He takes another step. He looks menacing. André retreats.

Come on . . . I'm sure you must have some sort of position on the question.

André No.

Man You don't agree with me? Is that it? Be honest, just tell me.

The Man's mobile rings. His tone changes.

54

Oh, will you excuse me? It's my associate . . . I absolutely have to take it . . . It's about a developing deal, and . . . Please be kind enough to excuse me.

He moves aside and goes to a corner of the room. André seems relieved. He looks around him.

Hello? No, no, I'm still down here . . .

Suddenly, Anne returns. The Man puts his hand in front of his mouth in an effort not to be heard.

(*On the phone.*) No, no, don't worry. I have the situation under control.

Anne I'm sorry, Dad.

André (*to Anne*) Where's your mother? Is she still in the garden? I don't see her . . .

He glances through the window again. He seems worried. The Man might eventually leave so as not to have his conversation in front of them.

Maybe she's gone out shopping. Don't you think? I haven't seen her this morning, it's a worry.

Anne Dad . . .

André What? I'm just wondering, that's all.

Pause.

Anne Here . . . I'm putting your coffee down over here. It's hot.

André I don't want coffee.

Anne But it's your breakfast.

André Is it morning?

Anne Yes.

André Oh? Right.

She puts the coffee down. He comes over to sit down and drink it.

And my croissants?

Anne They're here.

André Thank you. With –

Anne (*automatically interrupting him*) Strawberry jam, yes.

She sits down beside him. Pause. He seems happy.

All right? Are they the way you like them?

André Yes.

Anne Good.

Pause.

Dad . . . I wanted to talk to you . . .

André Yes?

Anne How shall I put it? You know . . . Your editor asked me to put your papers in order . . . Do you remember? A long time ago, you talked to him about some sort of private diary . . .

Pause.

I found it and read it.

André What?

Anne Your diary. I read it last night.

Pause.

I don't know if it's all true, but . . . I wanted to talk to you about it . . .

Pause.

The story about . . . that . . . that woman . . . The
German woman . . .

*The Man comes back into the room to look for
something in his jacket pocket, still on the phone.*

Man No, I told you, he's completely harmless now! It's
more or less in the bag! We'll be able to exchange in no
time.

*Anne and André watch the Man. What can he be
talking about? He disappears again.*

Anne I'd never have believed that . . . As far as I'm
concerned, you've always been a model . . . I mean . . .
You and Mum . . . A model of love . . . And . . . But in
the end, it's always the same story . . . It's ugly the way
stories all turn out the same. Even yours . . . Even yours,
Dad . . .

*She seems affected. There's a clear echo forming in her
mind of her discoveries about Pierre.*

André What?

Anne What's the story about Georges Dulon?

André You know, as time goes by, your attitude towards
certain things changes. What used to seem important to
us suddenly becomes trivial. Like an anecdote. You end
up forgetting about it. Soap bubbles. You put it into
perspective . . . You learn how to forgive . . .

Anne What are you talking about?

*She has a feeling something important is being said
between them. Once again the Man interrupts their
conversation.*

Man (*into the phone*) Tell the lawyer to stand by, OK?
And tell him the agreement still stands . . . He'll get his
share. Oh, yes, he'll get his share.

André What's he talking about?

Pause. Anne is looking for a way to resume their conversation.

Anne Anyway, about this private diary . . . I don't know what to do about it. You couldn't publish it, that much I understood. Because of Mum . . .

André Yes.

Anne You didn't want to hurt her.

André Who? Your mother?

Anne Yes. All that I understand. But what about now? I can't do anything without your agreement . . . What would you like me to do? Mm? What would you like me to do?

André Last night . . . Did you hear that storm?

Anne Last night? No, I thought it was the night before . . .

André No, no, it was last night . . . I didn't sleep well and . . . I had a strange dream . . . I couldn't understand what was going on . . . Everything felt precarious. Uncertain. Crumbling. Like walking across an abyss.

Anne An abyss?

André Yes. It was . . . frightening. And then I woke up. Luckily, I woke up . . . Imagine a dream you never wake up from . . . It'd be a real nightmare!

Suddenly, Madeleine appears in the doorway. She has a bag in her hand, as if she's just been out shopping.

Madeleine Here I am!

André gets up.

André Ah, there you are! Where have you been? I've been looking for you all morning.

Madeleine I went shopping for lunch . . . Did you sleep well?

André No. That's what I was just explaining . . .

Madeleine Must have been because of the storm.

André I'm sure.

Man (*into the phone*) I have to go. I'll keep you posted.

He hangs up.

Sorry.

Madeleine Good morning, Paul.

Man Good morning.

Madeleine Did you sleep well?

Man Very well. Thank you.

Anne You know they're not staying for lunch . . .

Madeleine (*frowning*) How come?

Anne They have to go.

Man Yes, I'm very sorry. We . . .

Madeleine You wouldn't like to leave after lunch?

Man We'd have loved to, but I have an important meeting at noon. I really can't postpone it.

Madeleine (*put out*) Oh? What a pity.

Man I know.

Anne All the more for us!

André What did you buy?

Madeleine Mushrooms.

André Ah . . . Wonderful. For lunch?

Madeleine (*as if stating the obvious*) Yes.

André Show me.

Madeleine shows them to him. It's a repeat of a fragment of an earlier scene.

Oh . . . Perfect . . . For years we didn't eat them. We preferred meat. I don't know what we were thinking.

Man I . . . Maybe I'll go and give her a hand.

Nobody knows who he's referring to.

Élise. Maybe I'll go and help her pack. Otherwise we're going to be late . . .

He goes out. Pause.

Madeleine What do you think of him?

Anne Dad?

Madeleine No. Him . . .

She indicates the Man.

Anne I don't know. Nice. Isn't he? You don't think so?

Madeleine shrugs her shoulders.

Madeleine The important thing is that your sister seems to see something in him.

Anne Yes.

Madeleine I wonder where she digs them up . . .

Brief pause.

Anne On the other hand, I don't think Dad looks well at all.

Madeleine Who?

Anne Dad.

Madeleine Oh, you're not going to start that again?

Anne Start what?

Madeleine You know very well. (*To André.*) Have you finished? You've hardly eaten a thing . . .

André I'm not hungry.

Madeleine You say that and in an hour's time, you'll come and tell me you're hungry . . . And you'll start snacking!

Madeleine takes away the breakfast things.

Anne I'm just giving you my opinion.

Madeleine I couldn't care less about your opinion!

Anne Why are you reacting like this?

Madeleine Because I can get on very well on my own! I don't need your advice.

Anne But I . . .

Madeleine groans. But Anne is determined to persist with this conversation.

All I'm saying is that Élise and I were disturbed to find out things weren't working out for him and . . .

Madeleine And what? Is that why you both came this weekend? To run an inspection?

Anne We're worried, Mum, that's all. We thought it must sometimes be a burden for you. Being here with him on your own . . .

Madeleine I just told you: we can get on very well on our own.

Anne All the same I think you ought to –

Madeleine (*interrupting her*) Did I ask your opinion? No! I mean, what's all this about? You turn up with your sister, you spend a couple of days here, and then you're suddenly experts on the way we ought to be living our lives?

Anne But . . .

Madeleine I know very well what you're cooking up. What do you think? You think I was born yesterday?

André What's . . .?

Anne Please, Mum . . . All I'm saying is there might be other solutions.

Madeleine Oh, yes? Go on, explain them to me . . . What are they?

André What's . . .?

Madeleine You want to have your father to live with you?

Brief pause. No answer.

That's what I thought. What then? You want to put him in a nursing home, is that it? I wish you'd just say things clearly. Is that what you want? You want to get rid of him?

Anne Why are you getting annoyed?

Madeleine Because I've seen through your little game.

Anne What little game?

Madeleine Your little schemes.

Anne What are you talking about?

Madeleine Right, that's enough now! When I need you, I'll send for you! In the meantime, fuck off! And if you're not happy about it, all you have to do is go back with your sister!

Madeleine leaves.

André What's the matter with her?

Anne Nothing.

André No. I heard . . . you were arguing.

Anne No, no. Don't worry.

André Was it about the mushrooms?

Élise comes in.

Élise What's going on?

Anne Nothing.

Élise Is there a problem?

Anne No. It's just . . .

Élise What?

Anne No, I think it's just the fact of being here. Everything's jumbled up in my head . . . Don't you find? I don't know. All these memories . . . These . . .

Élise Are you crying?

Anne No, no. Sorry.

Élise You take things too much to heart, Anne . . .

Anne But don't you have doubts?

Élise What about?

Anne The Blue House . . . I don't know . . . Do you really think it's the best solution?

Élise I can't see any alternative.

Anne I'm trying to imagine what Mum would have thought about it. I get the feeling I can see her glaring at me.

Élise She'd understand.

Anne I don't think she would.

Élise Yes, she would.

Anne No. She'd be furious. I can picture it very clearly . . . Believe me, she'd judge us very harshly. She'd curse us.

Élise What are you talking about?

Anne I know it. I can hear her now . . .

André turns to them.

André What's the matter, my little scorchers?

Élise Nothing, Dad.

André Have you been quarrelling again?

Anne No, no . . .

André Well? What's going on?

Élise I promise you, Dad. Everything's fine.

Anne We were just talking.

André Life's too short for arguments. Believe me.

Anne Yes, yes . . .

André It's short . . . Come on . . . Anne . . . Dry your tears . . . Mm? And make up. All right? My little darlings . . .

The Man arrives. He has a suitcase in his hand.

Man Sorry, I . . . I didn't want to disturb you, I . . . Where shall I put this?

Élise Leave it there for the minute.

He crosses the room and puts it by the front door.

André Sure you wouldn't like to have lunch with us before you go?

Élise It's nice of you, but . . .

André You'd make your mother very happy . . .

Anne Dad . . .

André What?

Pause. They're all hesitating.

Man (*to the daughters*) Aren't you going to say anything to him?

André What about?

Man How much longer is this going to go on?

Élise Stop it.

Man What?

André (*to his daughters*) What's he talking about?

Pause.

What's happening? Tell me.

Pause.

Is there a problem?

Pause. The Man spots a little square of cardboard on the floor. It must have fallen out of the bouquet. He picks it up.

Man Must have fallen out of the bouquet.

André What is that?

André takes it out of his hand and reads it.

Élise No!

André What is it?

It's a condolence card. Everyone watches him reading it. Pause. He slips it into a pocket, as if nothing had happened. His face remains expressionless, apparently at least. He stands in silence for a moment.

Anne Dad?

Pause.

Élise Dad?

Interminable pause.

Blackout.

Epilogue

Epilogue. A little later, André is at the window, as at the beginning of the play. Madeleine is sitting down. She's peeling the mushrooms. The suitcase has been left behind. It's still standing by the front door.

Madeleine I prefer it when they're gone. It's nice of them to come and see us . . . But after two days, I've had enough of it. Don't you think?

He doesn't answer.

I don't know how we put up with it all those years. I'm not saying I can't stand them. No, they're nice girls. Especially Élise . . . But they have their lives. And we have ours. Isn't that right? It's better when we don't mix them up. You disagree?

He smiles at her, as if to say she's right.

When it's just the two of us . . .

Pause.

In the end, Anne decided to go with them. Thank goodness. It's slightly my fault. I had a quarrel with her. Maybe I was a bit . . . You know me, I don't always pull my punches! But I can't bear people telling you what you ought or ought not to do . . .

Pause.

What are you looking at? Wouldn't you rather come and sit down?

He doesn't respond.

They don't understand the situation. They can't understand that we don't need anyone. Because we don't need anyone.

Don't you agree? We're fine just the two of us, aren't we? Why should we need to change anything?

Pause.

Just what is it you're looking at? They've been gone a long time. What's the use of staying stuck over there? Come and sit down beside me.

André smiles tenderly at her and comes over to sit next to her.

That's it.

Pause.

André Funny colour these mushrooms, don't you think?

Madeleine You think they're not edible?

André You're not planning to poison us?

She smiles. Pause.

Madeleine This morning, when I was doing the shopping, you know what I was thinking about? I was thinking about our wedding. You remember it?

André Yes.

Madeleine At the Lutetia.

André I can see your dress now, yes. Your smile . . . I can see our room . . . I can see our bed.

Madeleine In those days, you always used to recite poems to me. I was thinking about that just now and trying to remember . . . You know, something about an unknown bird . . .

André
    'At the height of the storm
    There's always a bird to reassure us,
    The unknown bird:
    It sings and then it flies away.'

Madeleine Yes. That's it. 'It sings and then it flies away...' Beautiful.

André Yes. Very beautiful.

Madeleine It was such a long time ago... They say life is short, but it isn't true. It's terribly long.

André Sometimes, it seems endless.

Madeleine Yes. But when it does end, it can only be a deliverance. Don't you think?

Pause.

Are you hungry? I'm not surprised, you hardly had any breakfast. It's always the same with you... I'm nearly finished. In a minute, we can sit at the table. Afterwards, if you like, we can go for a walk. Through the forest. That appeal to you? After that storm we had, it'll smell good... I have to be back about three o'clock, because Jean is coming to repaint the shutters. And you can have your siesta. While you're resting, I can do some work in my garden and –

André (*interrupting her*) What would I do without you?

Madeleine smiles at him. André remains serious. He's looking at her with some intensity.

What would I do? What would become of me without you?

Madeleine Don't worry. Here I am.

He doesn't look very convinced of this.

I'll always be here. Don't worry. I'm not going to let you down. You know very well I'm not the kind of person who doesn't keep her promises. Mm? You know that very well, don't you?

André Yes.

Madeleine So? Don't be afraid of anything. I'm taking care of you. I'm taking care of you, my darling boy . . .

She smiles at him. Pause. She goes on peeling the mushrooms. He fetches the little condolence card out of his pocket and reads it again. Suddenly, he takes her hand and squeezes it very hard – as if he was clinging on to her. Pause.

Blackout.